I'm Thinking of a Border State

Bela Davis

Abdo Kids Junior
is an Imprint of Abdo Kids
abdobooks.com

Abdo
I'M THINKING OF A STATE
Kids

abdobooks.com

Published by Abdo Kids, a division of ABDO, P.O. Box 398166, Minneapolis, Minnesota 55439.

Printed in the United States of America, North Mankato, Minnesota.

102025

012026

Photo Credits: Alamy, Getty Images, Shutterstock

Production Contributors: Teddy Borth, Jennie Forsberg, Grace Hansen

Design Contributors: Candice Keimig, Pakou Moua

Library of Congress Control Number: 2025936509

Publisher's Cataloging-in-Publication Data

Names: Davis, Bela, author.

Title: I'm thinking of a border state / by Bela Davis

Description: Minneapolis, Minnesota : Abdo Kids, 2026 | Series: I'm thinking of a state | Includes online resources and index.

Identifiers: ISBN 9798384907367 (lib. bdg.) | ISBN 9798384908067 (ebook) | ISBN 9798384908418 (Read-to-Me ebook)

Subjects: LCSH: Border States--Juvenile literature. | American states (United States)--Juvenile literature. | Geography--Juvenile literature. | Physical geography--United States--Juvenile literature.

Classification: DDC 917--dc23

Table of Contents

Guess the State!

I'm thinking of a border state. A border state touches a different country!

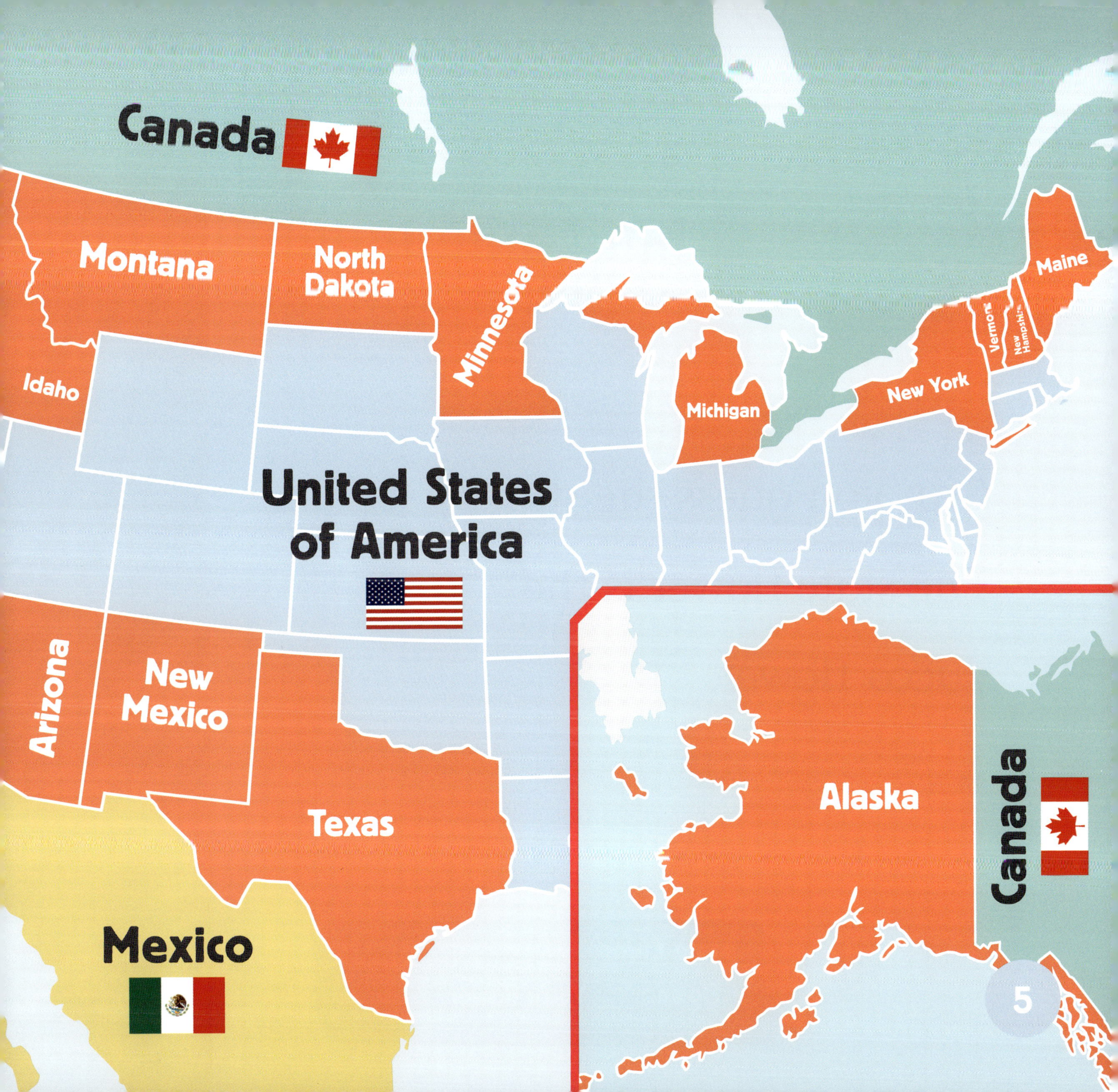
Canada
Montana
North Dakota
Minnesota
Maine
Idaho
Michigan
New York
United States of America
Arizona
New Mexico
Texas
Alaska
Canada
Mexico

Can you guess the state?

The state flower is the yucca flower.

State Clues

- **Flower:** Yucca flower

The state bird is the greater roadrunner.

State Clues

- **Flower:** Yucca flower
- **Bird:** Greater roadrunner

Rattlesnakes live in this state.

State Clues

- **Flower:** Yucca flower
- **Bird:** Greater roadrunner
- **Animal:** Rattlesnake

This state hosts a hot air balloon festival!

State Clues

- **Flower:** Yucca flower
- **Bird:** Greater roadrunner
- **Animal:** Rattlesnake
- **Activity:** Hot air balloon

770 KKO
NEWS

People can visit Roswell and try to find aliens.

State Clues

- **Flower:** Yucca flower
- **Bird:** Greater roadrunner
- **Animal:** Rattlesnake
- **Activity:** Hot air balloon
- **Visit:** Roswell

People explore caves at Carlsbad Caverns **National Park**!

State Clues

- **Flower:** Yucca flower
- **Bird:** Greater roadrunner
- **Animal:** Rattlesnake
- **Activity:** Hot air balloon
- **Visit:** Roswell
- **Explore:** Carlsbad Caverns

The state's capital is Santa Fe.

State Clues

- **Flower:** Yucca flower
- **Bird:** Greater roadrunner
- **Animal:** Rattlesnake
- **Activity:** Hot air balloon
- **Visit:** Roswell
- **Explore:** Carlsbad Caverns
- **Capital:** Santa Fe

Now you have all the clues! Can you guess what state I'm thinking of?

State Clues

- **Flower:** Yucca flower
- **Bird:** Greater roadrunner
- **Animal:** Rattlesnake
- **Activity:** Hot air balloon
- **Visit:** Roswell
- **Explore:** Carlsbad Caverns
- **Capital:** Santa Fe

NM
AZ
CA
TX

I'm Thinking of...
New Mexico!

Glossary

festival

a celebration that repeats, often once a year, and involves special activities or amusements.

national park

a special area of land that is set aside by the United States government to protect it.

Index

Visit **abdokids.com** to access crafts, games, videos, and more!

Use Abdo Kids code

IIK7367

or scan this QR code!